A SLOTH'S GUIDE TO MINDFULNESS

BY TON MAK

CHRONICLE BOOKS
SAN FRANCISCO

Library of Congress Cataloging-in-Publication Data

Names: Mak, Ton, author.
Title: A Sloth's guide to mindfulness / by Ton Mak.
Description: San Francisco : Chronicle Books, [2018]
Identifiers: LCCN 2017049263 | ISBN 9781452169460
(hardcover : alk. paper)
Subjects: LCSH: Emotions. | Awareness. | Meditation—Buddhism.
Classification: LCC BF531 .M263 2018 | DDC 158.1/3—dc23 LC
record available at https://lccn.loc.gov/2017049263

Manufactured in China

MIX
Paper from
responsible sources
FSC™ C008047

Designed by Allison Weiner and Ton Mak

10 9 8 7 6 5 4 3

Chronicle Books LLC
680 Second Street
San Francisco, California 94107
www.chroniclebooks.com

This book is dedicated to my mother Audrey, who guided my first meditation session when I was a small bean of a child.

Sometimes it's hard being a sloth.

Life feels a bit slow.

It takes a big effort to get small things done.

One hour later . . .

Getting out of bed seems impossible.

Work seems endless.

Our thoughts race at rocket speed.

Slowing down is hard.

But trying to do everything is even harder.

Some days, everything is annoying.

We forget the small happy things.
Happy things that are already within us
and around us.

Practicing mindfulness reveals the happiness in the present.

Being mindful brings awareness
of the wonders around us.

We can see more clearly in the present by emptying our minds.

Mindfulness has no time restrictions.

It spreads through all mundane experiences.

The search for mindfulness is not
marked by success.
Some days will be harder than others.
The key is not to try too hard.

If we focus too hard on results,
it becomes harder to stay present.

Being in the moment, we can identify
our fear, anger, and doubt, and become
more aware of these feelings.

There is no need to run or hide from them.

Befriend your emotions—the good ones
and the bad ones.

Negative feels come and go.
It's OK to wait them out.

Relax.

Watch.

Reflect.

Hang in there.

Sometimes just taking pause for five minutes
is the best practice.

Empty your mind, like a deflating balloon.

Visualize washing away all your stresses
and negative thoughts.

WOOOOOOSH.

Visualize resting on a snug branch.

Light and relaxed.

If your mind is still racing . . .

don't give up.

boo

Take a walk in the sun.

Give nature a big
fat hug.

Laugh it off.

HUR
HUR
HUR

Show small acts of kindness.

Be thankful.

.

When we live consciously
our happiness expands.

When eating, eat slowly.
Enjoy every bite.

When talking, pause to listen intently to others.

When walking,
walk mindfully.

No rush.

Focus on the present moment.

It's OK to not be productive all the time.
It's OK to pause.

Meditate.

Sitting cross-legged is a good starting point.
But really, do what feels right.

Curl up into a nugget.

Stand straight.

Lie down.

You do you.

Find peace by finding your center.
Gently close your eyes.
Settle into your comfort zone.

Check in with how you are feeling.
Is there any pain?

How does your breath feel?

Bring awareness to your body.

Observe any contact your body is making with the ground.

Notice the feeling of your breath coming in and out.

Notice the feeling of your belly as it expands and falls with each breath.

Focus on deep breathing.

Inhale.

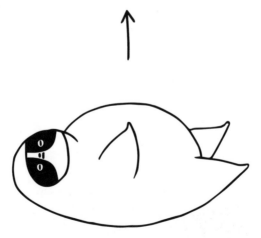

Exhale.

Imagine your breath running through your body.

No frowning. Smile.

If your mind wanders, try focusing on:
    the silence around you
    your space and surroundings
    your breathing

Be aware of your thoughts, but do not dwell on them.

You might be distracted by an intense feeling.

Gently redirect your attention back to the sensations of your body and your breath.

It's impossible to stop all thoughts.
So leave everything as it is.
Eventually they will pass.

When you wish to return to the day, gently
open your eyes.

Slowly move forward.
Slow is OK.

Enjoy all the wonderful things around you.

Some final sloth words . . .

Dream big.
Work hard.

But remember to give yourself a break.
Drink some tea . . .

sing a little . . .

float in the ocean . . .

. . . or just sit someplace nice.

Don't be afraid of
making mistakes.

Life can be an adventure if you don't hold yourself back.

Stand up for yourself.
Go at your own pace.

Listen to your heart.

And always appreciate the current view.

ACKNOWLEDGMENTS

A big thank you to the wonderful team at Chronicle Books for having so much love and belief in the Sloth: Camaren Subhiyah, Deanne Katz, and Allison Weiner.

And thank you to my family, loved ones, and my supportive studio cats Benji and Dusty.

ABOUT THE AUTHOR

Ton Mak is a visual artist and writer.
Her specialty lies in a series of bouncy, friendly, and often chubby creatures known as FLABJACKS. Ton likes sloths, sweet potatoes, and hot tea. For more happy happenings, visit www.flabjacks.com.